Pasta Perfection The Ultimate Guide to Cool and Flavorful Pasta Salads

Discover the Art of Crafting 100 Irresistible Pasta Salads for Every Occasion

PHILIP MANN

Copyright Material ©2025

All Rights Reserved

No part of this book may be used or transmitted in any form or by any means without the proper written consent of the publisher and copyright owner, except for brief quotations used in a review. This book should not be considered a substitute for medical, legal, or other professional advice.

TABLE OF CONTENTS

- TABLE OF CONTENTS 3
- INTRODUCTION 6
- **CHEESY PASTA SALADS** 7
  - 1. Saucy Cheddar Fusilli Salad 8
  - 2. Minty Feta and Orzo Salad 10
  - 3. Cheesy Pepperoni Rotini Salad 12
  - 4. Gorgonzola Pasta Salad 14
  - 5. Romano Linguine Pasta Salad 16
  - 6. Minty Feta and Orzo Salad 18
  - 7. Nutty Gorgonzola Pasta Salad 20
  - 8. Fresh Lemon Pasta Salad 22
  - 9. Classic Macaroni and Cheese Pasta Salad 24
  - 10. Three-Cheese Tortellini Salad 26
  - 11. Pesto and Sun-Dried Tomato Penne Salad 28
  - 12. Cheddar and Broccoli Bowtie Pasta Salad 30
  - 13. Greek Orzo Salad with Feta 32
- **GRILLED PASTA SALADS** 34
  - 14. Grilled Veggie Fusilli Pasta Salad 35
  - 15. Grilled Vegetable and Pesto Pasta Salad 37
  - 16. Grilled Chicken Caesar Pasta Salad 39
  - 17. Grilled Shrimp and Avocado Pasta Salad 41
  - 18. Grilled Summer Vegetable and Feta Pasta Salad 43
  - 19. Grilled Corn and Black Bean Pasta Salad 45
  - 20. Grilled Chicken and Pesto Tortellini Salad 47
  - 21. Grilled Vegetable and Feta Orzo Salad 49
  - 22. Grilled Tofu and Sesame Noodle Salad 51
  - 23. Grilled Swordfish and Orzo Salad 53
  - 24. Grilled Scallop and Asparagus Pasta Salad 55
- **FISH AND SEAFOOD PASTA SALAD** 57
  - 25. Tuna and Artichoke Pasta Salad 58
  - 26. Shrimp and Avocado Pasta Salad 60
  - 27. Smoked Salmon and Dill Pasta Salad 62
  - 28. Crab and Mango Pasta Salad 64
  - 29. Scallop and Asparagus Pasta Salad 66
  - 30. Lemon Garlic Shrimp and Orzo Salad 68
  - 31. Grilled Tuna and White Bean Pasta Salad 70
  - 32. Cilantro Lime Salmon Pasta Salad 72
  - 33. Lobster and Mango Pasta Salad 74

34. MEDITERRANEAN TZATZIKI SHRIMP PASTA SALAD 76
35. SHRIMP AND CHERRY TOMATO PASTA SALAD 78
36. NUTTY TUNA AND PASTA SALAD 81

POULTRY PASTA SALAD 83

37. CHICKEN TENDERS & FARFALLE SALAD 84
38. CREAMY PENN PASTA SALAD 86
39. FETA AND ROASTED TURKEY SALAD 88
40. NUTTY CHICKEN PASTA SALAD 90
41. CHICKEN CAESAR PASTA SALAD 92
42. TURKEY AND CRANBERRY PASTA SALAD 94
43. LEMON HERB GRILLED CHICKEN PASTA SALAD 96
44. RANCH CHICKEN AND BACON PASTA SALAD 98
45. CURRY CHICKEN AND MANGO PASTA SALAD 100
46. GREEK CHICKEN AND ORZO SALAD 102
47. CHICKEN AND BLACK BEAN PASTA SALAD 104
48. MANGO CURRY CHICKEN PASTA SALAD 106
49. CAPRESE CHICKEN PESTO PASTA SALAD 108
50. ASIAN SESAME CHICKEN NOODLE SALAD 110
51. LEMON HERB TURKEY AND ASPARAGUS PASTA SALAD 112
52. CHICKEN AND BROCCOLI PESTO PASTA SALAD 114
53. BUFFALO CHICKEN PASTA SALAD 116
54. CRANBERRY WALNUT CHICKEN PASTA SALAD 118

COLD MEATS PASTA SALAD 120

55. ITALIAN COLD PASTA SALAD WITH SALAMI 121
56. TURKEY AND CRANBERRY COLD PASTA SALAD 123
57. COLD PASTA SALAD WITH HAM AND CHEDDAR 125
58. CHICKEN CAESAR COLD PASTA SALAD 127
59. GREEK ORZO PASTA SALAD WITH GYRO MEAT 129
60. ROAST BEEF AND CHEDDAR PASTA SALAD 131
61. BACON RANCH COLD CHICKEN PASTA SALAD 133
62. ITALIAN ANTIPASTO PASTA SALAD 135
63. SMOKED TURKEY AND AVOCADO PASTA SALAD 137
64. GRILLED SAUSAGE AND VEGETABLE PASTA SALAD 139
65. SHRIMP AND AVOCADO COLD PASTA SALAD 141
66. PASTRAMI AND SWISS COLD PASTA SALAD 143
67. TUNA AND WHITE BEAN COLD PASTA SALAD 145
68. BBQ CHICKEN AND CORN PASTA SALAD 147
69. ITALIAN SAUSAGE AND PEPPERS PASTA SALAD 149
70. COPYCAT RUBY TUESDAY PASTA SALAD 151

VEGGIE PASTA SALAD 153

71. VEGAN RIGATONI BASIL SALAD 154
72. BLT PASTA SALAD 156
73. MACARONI COLESLAW 158

74. Kalamata Rotini Salad 160
75. Tortellini Jarred Salad 162
76. Garlic-Mushroom Fusilli with Pear Salad 164
77. Mediterranean Vegetable Pasta Salad 166
78. Pesto Veggie Spiral Pasta Salad 168
79. Rainbow Veggie Pasta Salad 170
80. Asian Sesame Vegetable Noodle Salad 172
81. Caprese Vegetable Pasta Salad 174
82. Greek Orzo Vegetable Salad 176
83. Roasted Vegetable and Chickpea Pasta Salad 178
84. Spinach and Artichoke Cold Pasta Salad 180
85. Thai Peanut Vegetable Noodle Salad 182
86. Caesar Veggie Pasta Salad 184

COLD FRUITY PASTA SALADS 186

87. Tropical Fruit and Shrimp Pasta Salad 187
88. Berry and Feta Pasta Salad 189
89. Citrus and Avocado Pasta Salad 191
90. Watermelon and Feta Pasta Salad 193
91. Mango and Black Bean Pasta Salad 195
92. Apple and Walnut Pasta Salad 197
93. Pineapple and Ham Pasta Salad 199
94. Citrus Berry Pasta Salad 201
95. Kiwi, Strawberry, and Rotini Pasta Salad 203
96. Mango Salsa with Farfalle Pasta Salad 205
97. Peach and Prosciutto Pasta Salad 207
98. Blueberry and Goat Cheese Pasta Salad 209
99. Spinach, Pea, Raspberry, and Spiral Pasta Salad 211
100. Mandarin Orange and Almond Pasta Salad 213

CONCLUSION 215

INTRODUCTION

Pasta salads are the perfect fusion of simplicity, flavor, and versatility—ideal for every season and any gathering. *Pasta Perfection The Ultimate Guide to Cool and Flavorful Pasta Salads* is your go-to cookbook for mastering the art of fresh, vibrant, and delicious pasta salads that will elevate your meals with ease.

With 100 carefully curated recipes, this book offers a variety of combinations, from Mediterranean-inspired delights and zesty Asian twists to creamy classic favorites and bold, unexpected creations. Whether you're preparing a refreshing side dish for a summer picnic, a hearty meal-prep option for busy weekdays, or a show-stopping salad for a festive gathering, you'll find endless inspiration in these pages.

Learn how to balance flavors, choose the best pasta shapes, and experiment with homemade dressings and exciting ingredient pairings. With easy-to-follow instructions and creative variations, this book will help you turn simple pasta salads into culinary masterpieces. Get ready to transform your everyday meals with the cool, crisp, and mouthwatering magic of pasta perfection!

CHEESY PASTA SALADS

1. Saucy Cheddar Fusilli Salad

INGREDIENTS:
- 2 Tablespoons olive oil
- 6 green onions, chopped
- 1 teaspoons salt
- 3/4 cup chopped pickled jalapeno peppers
- 1 (16 oz.) package fusilli pasta
- 1 (2.25 oz.) can slice black olives
- 2 lb. extra lean ground beef
- 1 (1.25 oz.) package taco seasoning mix
- 1 (8 oz.) package shredded Cheddar cheese
- 1 (24 oz.) jar mild salsa
- 1 (8 oz.) bottle ranch dressing
- 1 1/2 red bell peppers, chopped

INSTRUCTIONS:
a) Place a large pot over medium heat. Fill it with water and stir into it the olive oil with salt.
b) Cook it until it starts boiling.
c) Add the pasta and boil it for 10 min. Remove it from the water and place it aside to drain.
d) Place a large pan over medium heat. Brown in it the beef for 12 min. Discard the excess grease.
e) Add the taco seasoning and mix them well. Place the mix aside to lose heat completely.
f) Get a large mixing bowl: Mix in it the salsa, ranch dressing, bell peppers, green onions, jalapenos, and black olives.
g) Add the pasta with cooked beef, Cheddar cheese, and dressing mix. Stir them well. Place a piece of plastic wrap over the salad bowl. Place it in the fridge for 1 h 15 min.

2.Minty Feta and Orzo Salad

INGREDIENTS:
- 1 1/4 cup orzo pasta
- 1 small red onion, diced
- 6 Tablespoons olive oil, divided
- 1/2 cup finely chopped fresh mint leaves
- 3/4 cup dried brown lentils, rinsed
- 1/2 cup chopped fresh dill
- salt and pepper to taste
- 1/3 cup red wine vinegar
- 3 cloves garlic, minced
- 1/2 cup Kalamata olives, pitted and chopped
- 1 1/2 cup crumbled feta cheese

INSTRUCTIONS:
a) Cook the pasta according to the instructions on the package.
b) Bring a salted large saucepan of water to a boil. Cook in it the lentils until it starts boiling.
c) Lower the heat and put it on the lid. Cook the lentils for 22 min. Remove them from the water.
d) Get a small mixing bowl: Combine in it the olive oil, vinegar, and garlic. Whisk them well to make the dressing.
e) Get a large mixing bowl: Toss in it the lentils, dressing, olives, feta cheese, red onion, mint, and dill, with salt and pepper.
f) Wrap a plastic wrap on the salad bowl and place it in the fridge for 2 h 30 min. Adjust the seasoning of the salad then serve it.

3.Cheesy Pepperoni Rotini Salad

INGREDIENTS:
- 1 (16 oz.) package tri-color rotini pasta
- 1 (8 oz.) package mozzarella cheese
- 1/4 lb. sliced pepperoni sausage
- 1 cup fresh broccoli florets
- 1 (16 oz.) bottle Italian-style salad
- 1 (6 oz.) can black olives, drained
- dressing

INSTRUCTIONS:
a) Cook the pasta according to the instructions on the package.
b) Get a large mixing bowl: Toss in it the pasta, pepperoni, broccoli, olives, cheese, and dressing.
c) Adjust the seasoning of the salad and place it in the fridge for 1 h 10 min. Serve it.

4.Gorgonzola Pasta Salad

INGREDIENTS:
- 1 (16 oz.) package penne pasta
- 1/2 cup canola oil
- 2 tablespoons canola oil
- 1/4 cup walnut oil
- 2 C. fresh spinach - rinsed, dried and torn into bite size pieces
- 1/3 cup champagne vinegar
- 2 tablespoons honey
- 1 small green bell pepper, cut into 1 inch pieces
- 2 C. crumbled Gorgonzola cheese
- 1 C. chopped walnuts
- 1 small red bell pepper, cut into 1 inch pieces
- 1 small yellow bell pepper, cut into 1 inch pieces

INSTRUCTIONS:
a) Cook the pasta according to the instructions on the package.
b) Place a large pan over medium heat. Cook in it the spinach with a splash of water for 2 to 3 min or until it wilts.
c) Get a large mixing bowl: Toss in it the spinach, green pepper, red pepper, yellow pepper and cooled pasta.
d) Get a small mixing bowl: Combine in it the 1/2 cup canola oil, walnut oil, vinegar and honey. Mix them well.
e) Drizzle the dressing over the pasta salad. Top it with walnuts and gorgonzola cheese then serve it.

5. Romano Linguine Pasta Salad

INGREDIENTS:
- 1 (8 oz.) package linguine pasta
- 1/2 teaspoons red pepper flakes
- 1 (12 oz.) bag broccoli florets, cut into bite size pieces
- 1/4 teaspoons ground black pepper
- salt to taste
- 1/4 cup olive oil
- 4 teaspoons minced garlic
- 1/2 cup finely shredded Romano cheese
- 2 Tablespoons finely chopped fresh flat-leaf parsley

INSTRUCTIONS:
a) Cook the pasta according to the instructions on the package.
b) Bring a pot of water to a boil. Place a steamer on top. Steam in it the broccoli with the lid on for 6 min
c) Place a saucepan over medium heat. Heat the oil in it. Sauté in it the garlic with pepper flakes for 2 min.
d) Get a large mixing bowl: Transfer to it the sautéed garlic mix with pasta, broccoli, Romano cheese, parsley, black pepper, and salt. Mix them well.
e) Adjust the seasoning of the salad. Serve it right away.
f) Enjoy.

6. Minty Feta and Orzo Salad

INGREDIENTS:
- 1 1/4 cup orzo pasta
- 1 small red onion, diced
- 6 tablespoons olive oil, divided
- 1/2 cup finely chopped fresh mint leaves
- 3/4 cup dried brown lentils, rinsed and drained
- 1/2 cup chopped fresh dill
- salt and pepper to taste
- 1/3 cup red wine vinegar
- 3 cloves garlic, minced
- 1/2 cup Kalamata olives, pitted and chopped
- 1 1/2 cup crumbled feta cheese

INSTRUCTIONS:
a) Cook the pasta according to the instructions on the package.
b) Bring a salted large saucepan of water to a boil. Cook in it the lentils until it starts boiling.
c) Lower the heat and put on the lid. Cook the lentils for 22 minutes. Remove them from the water.
d) Get a small mixing bowl: Combine in it the olive oil, vinegar, and garlic. Whisk them well to make the dressing.
e) Get a large mixing bowl: Toss in it the lentils, dressing, olives, feta cheese, red onion, mint, and dill, with salt and pepper.
f) Wrap a plastic wrap on the salad bowl and place it in the fridge for 2 h 30 minutes. Adjust the seasoning of the salad then serve it.
g) Enjoy.

7.Nutty Gorgonzola Pasta Salad

INGREDIENTS:
- 2 lb. sirloin tips, cubed
- 1/2 cup red wine
- 1/2 yellow onion, chopped
- 1 (1.25 oz.) package beef with onion soup mix
- 2 (10.75 oz.) cans condensed cream of mushroom soup
- 2 (16 oz.) packages egg noodles
- 1 cup milk

INSTRUCTIONS:
a) Heat a large skillet on medium-high heat and stir fry the beef and onion for about 5
b) minutes.
c) Meanwhile in a bowl, mix together the mushroom soup, wine, milk and soup mix.
d) Place the mixture in the skillet and bring to a simmer.
e) Reduce heat to low and simmer, covered for about 2 hours.
f) Reduce heat to its lowest setting and simmer, covered for about 4 hours.
g) In a large pan of lightly salted boiling water, cook the egg noodles for about 5 minutes.
h) Drain well.
i) Place the beef mixture over the noodles and serve.

8. Fresh Lemon Pasta Salad

INGREDIENTS:
- 1 (16 oz.) package tri-color rotini pasta
- 1 pinch salt and ground black pepper to taste
- 2 tomatoes, seeded and diced
- 2 cucumbers - peeled, seeded, and diced
- 1 avocado, diced
- 1 squeeze lemon juice
- 1 (4 oz.) can sliced black olives
- 1/2 cup Italian dressing, or more to taste
- 1/2 cup shredded Parmesan cheese

INSTRUCTIONS:
a) Cook the pasta according to the instructions on the package.
b) Get a large mixing bowl: Combine in it the pasta, tomatoes, cucumbers, olives, Italian dressing, Parmesan cheese, salt, and pepper. Stir them well.
c) Place the pasta in the fridge for 1 h 15 minutes.
d) Get a small mixing bowl: Stir in it the lemon juice with avocado. Toss the avocado with pasta salad then serve it.
e) Enjoy.

9. Classic Macaroni and Cheese Pasta Salad

INGREDIENTS:
- 2 cups elbow macaroni, cooked and cooled
- 1 cup sharp cheddar cheese, cubed
- 1/2 cup mayonnaise
- 1/4 cup sour cream
- 1 tablespoon Dijon mustard
- 1/2 teaspoon garlic powder
- Salt and pepper to taste
- Chopped fresh parsley for garnish (optional)

INSTRUCTIONS:
a) In a large bowl, combine cooked macaroni and cheddar cheese cubes.
b) In a separate bowl, mix together mayonnaise, sour cream, Dijon mustard, and garlic powder.
c) Pour the dressing over the macaroni and cheese, tossing to coat evenly.
d) Season with salt and pepper to taste.
e) Garnish with chopped fresh parsley if desired.
f) Chill in the refrigerator for at least 1 hour before serving.

10. Three-Cheese Tortellini Salad

INGREDIENTS:
- 1 lb tri-color cheese tortellini, cooked and cooled
- 1 cup mozzarella cheese, cubed
- 1/2 cup feta cheese, crumbled
- 1/4 cup grated Parmesan cheese
- 1 cup cherry tomatoes, halved
- 1/4 cup red onion, finely chopped
- 1/4 cup fresh basil, chopped
- 1/3 cup balsamic vinaigrette dressing

INSTRUCTIONS:
a) In a large bowl, combine tortellini, mozzarella, feta, Parmesan, cherry tomatoes, red onion, and fresh basil.
b) Drizzle the balsamic vinaigrette over the salad and toss to combine.
c) Refrigerate for at least 1 hour before serving.

11. Pesto and Sun-Dried Tomato Penne Salad

INGREDIENTS:
- 2 cups penne pasta, cooked and cooled
- 1/2 cup sun-dried tomatoes, chopped
- 1/2 cup shredded Parmesan cheese
- 1/3 cup pine nuts, toasted
- 1 cup baby spinach
- 1/2 cup pesto sauce
- Salt and pepper to taste

INSTRUCTIONS:
a) In a large bowl, combine penne pasta, sun-dried tomatoes, Parmesan cheese, pine nuts, and baby spinach.
b) Add the pesto sauce and toss until everything is well coated.
c) Season with salt and pepper to taste.
d) Chill in the refrigerator for at least 1 hour before serving.

12. Cheddar and Broccoli Bowtie Pasta Salad

INGREDIENTS:
- 2 cups bowtie pasta, cooked and cooled
- 1 cup sharp cheddar cheese, shredded
- 1 cup broccoli florets, blanched and chopped
- 1/4 cup red onion, finely chopped
- 1/2 cup mayonnaise
- 2 tablespoons white vinegar
- 1 tablespoon sugar
- Salt and pepper to taste

INSTRUCTIONS:
a) In a large bowl, combine bowtie pasta, cheddar cheese, broccoli, and red onion.
b) In a separate bowl, whisk together mayonnaise, white vinegar, sugar, salt, and pepper.
c) Pour the dressing over the pasta mixture and toss until evenly coated.
d) Refrigerate for at least 1 hour before serving.

13. Greek Orzo Salad with Feta

INGREDIENTS:
- 1 cup orzo pasta, cooked and cooled
- 1/2 cup feta cheese, crumbled
- 1 cup cucumber, diced
- 1 cup cherry tomatoes, halved
- 1/4 cup red onion, finely chopped
- 1/4 cup Kalamata olives, sliced
- 1/4 cup fresh parsley, chopped
- 1/3 cup Greek salad dressing

INSTRUCTIONS:
a) In a large bowl, combine orzo pasta, feta cheese, cucumber, cherry tomatoes, red onion, olives, and fresh parsley.
b) Drizzle the Greek salad dressing over the salad and toss to combine.
c) Refrigerate for at least 1 hour before serving.

GRILLED PASTA SALADS

14. Grilled Veggie Fusilli Pasta Salad

INGREDIENTS:
PASTA SALAD
- 1 pound fusilli
- 2 cups diced grilled red and yellow bell peppers
- 2 cups halved cherry tomatoes
- 2 cups diced grilled onion
- 2 cups red wine vinaigrette

RED WINE VINAIGRETTE
- 1 cup extra virgin olive oil
- ⅓ red wine vinegar
- 2 tablespoons water
- 4 cloves garlic, finely grated
- 2 teaspoons Dijon mustard
- 2 teaspoons dried oregano
- 2 teaspoons granulated onion
- 1 pinch crushed chili flakes
- 2 teaspoons kosher salt
- 1 teaspoon freshly ground black pepper
- 2 tablespoons honey

INSTRUCTIONS
RED WINE VINAIGRETTE:
a) Combine all the ingredients in a container with a tight-fitting lid.
b) Shake well and store in the fridge until needed.

PASTA SALAD
c) Prepare pasta as directed on the package.
d) After cooking, strain the fusilli and cool it off in cold water to stop the cooking process.
e) Transfer the pasta to a sizable bowl and mix in the remaining ingredients.
f) Mix thoroughly, then leave overnight.

15. Grilled Vegetable and Pesto Pasta Salad

INGREDIENTS:
- 2 cups fusilli pasta, cooked and cooled
- 1 zucchini, sliced
- 1 red bell pepper, sliced
- 1 yellow bell pepper, sliced
- 1 cup cherry tomatoes, halved
- 1/2 cup red onion, thinly sliced
- 1/4 cup pesto sauce
- 2 tablespoons olive oil
- Salt and pepper to taste
- Grated Parmesan cheese for garnish

INSTRUCTIONS:
a) Toss zucchini, red and yellow bell peppers with olive oil, salt, and pepper.
b) Grill the vegetables until they have grill marks and are tender.
c) In a large bowl, combine pasta, grilled vegetables, cherry tomatoes, and red onion.
d) Add pesto sauce and toss until evenly coated.
e) Garnish with grated Parmesan cheese.
f) Refrigerate for at least 1 hour before serving.

16. Grilled Chicken Caesar Pasta Salad

INGREDIENTS:
- 2 cups penne pasta, cooked and cooled
- 1 lb chicken breast, grilled and sliced
- 1 cup cherry tomatoes, halved
- 1/2 cup black olives, sliced
- 1/4 cup red onion, finely chopped
- 1/2 cup Caesar dressing
- 1/4 cup grated Parmesan cheese
- Fresh parsley for garnish

INSTRUCTIONS:
a) Grill chicken breast until fully cooked, then slice it.
b) In a large bowl, combine pasta, grilled chicken, cherry tomatoes, black olives, and red onion.
c) Add Caesar dressing and toss until well combined.
d) Sprinkle grated Parmesan cheese and garnish with fresh parsley.
e) Refrigerate for at least 1 hour before serving.

17. Grilled Shrimp and Avocado Pasta Salad

INGREDIENTS:
- 2 cups rotini pasta, cooked and cooled
- 1 lb large shrimp, grilled
- 1 avocado, diced
- 1 cup cherry tomatoes, halved
- 1/4 cup red onion, finely chopped
- 1/4 cup cilantro, chopped
- Juice of 2 limes
- 2 tablespoons olive oil
- Salt and pepper to taste

INSTRUCTIONS:
a) Grill shrimp until they are opaque and have grill marks.
b) In a large bowl, combine pasta, grilled shrimp, diced avocado, cherry tomatoes, red onion, and cilantro.
c) Drizzle with lime juice and olive oil, then season with salt and pepper.
d) Toss until well combined.
e) Refrigerate for at least 1 hour before serving.

18. Grilled Summer Vegetable and Feta Pasta Salad

INGREDIENTS:
- 2 cups farfalle pasta, cooked and cooled
- 1 eggplant, sliced
- 2 zucchinis, sliced
- 1 cup cherry tomatoes, halved
- 1/2 cup crumbled feta cheese
- 1/4 cup fresh basil, chopped
- 3 tablespoons balsamic vinaigrette
- Salt and pepper to taste

INSTRUCTIONS:
a) Toss eggplant and zucchini slices with olive oil, salt, and pepper.
b) Grill the vegetables until they have grill marks and are tender.
c) In a large bowl, combine pasta, grilled vegetables, cherry tomatoes, feta cheese, and fresh basil.
d) Drizzle with balsamic vinaigrette and toss until well coated.
e) Refrigerate for at least 1 hour before serving.

19. Grilled Corn and Black Bean Pasta Salad

INGREDIENTS:
- 2 cups bowtie pasta, cooked and cooled
- 2 ears of corn, grilled and kernels removed
- 1 can (15 oz) black beans, rinsed and drained
- 1 red bell pepper, diced
- 1/4 cup red onion, finely chopped
- 1/4 cup fresh cilantro, chopped
- Juice of 2 limes
- 3 tablespoons olive oil
- 1 teaspoon cumin
- Salt and pepper to taste

INSTRUCTIONS:
a) Grill corn until kernels have a nice char, then remove the kernels.
b) In a large bowl, combine pasta, grilled corn, black beans, red bell pepper, red onion, and cilantro.
c) In a small bowl, whisk together lime juice, olive oil, cumin, salt, and pepper.
d) Pour the dressing over the pasta mixture and toss until well combined.
e) Refrigerate for at least 1 hour before serving.

20. Grilled Chicken and Pesto Tortellini Salad

INGREDIENTS:
- 2 cups tri-color tortellini, cooked and cooled
- 1 lb grilled chicken breast, sliced
- 1 cup cherry tomatoes, halved
- 1/2 cup roasted red peppers, chopped
- 1/4 cup pine nuts, toasted
- 1/2 cup fresh mozzarella balls
- 1/3 cup basil pesto
- 3 tablespoons extra-virgin olive oil
- Salt and pepper to taste

INSTRUCTIONS:
a) In a large bowl, combine tortellini, grilled chicken, cherry tomatoes, roasted red peppers, pine nuts, and mozzarella balls.
b) In a small bowl, whisk together basil pesto and olive oil.
c) Pour the dressing over the pasta mixture and toss until well coated.
d) Season with salt and pepper to taste.
e) Refrigerate for at least 1 hour before serving.

21. Grilled Vegetable and Feta Orzo Salad

INGREDIENTS:
- 2 cups orzo pasta, cooked and cooled
- 1 zucchini, sliced and grilled
- 1 red bell pepper, grilled and chopped
- 1 yellow bell pepper, grilled and chopped
- 1/2 cup red onion, grilled and finely chopped
- 1/2 cup crumbled feta cheese
- 1/4 cup fresh basil, chopped
- 3 tablespoons balsamic vinaigrette
- Salt and pepper to taste

INSTRUCTIONS:
a) Grill zucchini, red bell pepper, and red onion until they have grill marks.
b) In a large bowl, combine orzo pasta, grilled vegetables, feta cheese, and fresh basil.
c) Drizzle with balsamic vinaigrette and toss until well combined.
d) Season with salt and pepper to taste.
e) Refrigerate for at least 1 hour before serving.

22. Grilled Tofu and Sesame Noodle Salad

INGREDIENTS:
- 2 cups soba noodles, cooked and cooled
- 1 block extra-firm tofu, grilled and cubed
- 1 cup snap peas, blanched and sliced
- 1/2 cup shredded carrots
- 1/4 cup green onions, chopped
- 2 tablespoons sesame seeds, toasted
- 1/3 cup soy sauce
- 2 tablespoons sesame oil
- 1 tablespoon rice vinegar
- 1 tablespoon honey

INSTRUCTIONS:
a) Grill tofu until it has grill marks, then cube it.
b) In a large bowl, combine soba noodles, grilled tofu, snap peas, shredded carrots, green onions, and sesame seeds.
c) In a small bowl, whisk together soy sauce, sesame oil, rice vinegar, and honey.
d) Pour the dressing over the noodle mixture and toss until well coated.
e) Refrigerate for at least 1 hour before serving.

23. Grilled Swordfish and Orzo Salad

INGREDIENTS:
- 2 cups orzo pasta, cooked and cooled
- 1 lb swordfish steak, grilled and flaked
- 1 cup cherry tomatoes, halved
- 1/2 cup cucumber, diced
- 1/4 cup Kalamata olives, sliced
- 1/4 cup red onion, finely chopped
- 1/2 cup crumbled feta cheese
- 1/3 cup Greek dressing
- Fresh oregano for garnish
- Salt and pepper to taste

INSTRUCTIONS:
a) Grill swordfish steak until fully cooked, then flake it.
b) In a large bowl, combine orzo pasta, grilled swordfish, cherry tomatoes, cucumber, Kalamata olives, red onion, and feta cheese.
c) Add Greek dressing and toss until well mixed.
d) Garnish with fresh oregano.
e) Refrigerate for at least 1 hour before serving.

24.Grilled Scallop and Asparagus Pasta Salad

INGREDIENTS:
- 2 cups bowtie pasta, cooked and cooled
- 1 lb scallops, grilled
- 1 cup asparagus, grilled and chopped
- 1/4 cup sun-dried tomatoes, chopped
- 1/4 cup fresh basil, chopped
- 3 tablespoons extra-virgin olive oil
- Juice of 2 lemons
- Salt and pepper to taste

INSTRUCTIONS:
a) Grill scallops until they have grill marks.
b) Grill asparagus until tender and chop into bite-sized pieces.
c) In a large bowl, combine pasta, grilled scallops, grilled asparagus, sun-dried tomatoes, and fresh basil.
d) In a small bowl, whisk together olive oil and lemon juice.
e) Pour the dressing over the pasta mixture and toss until well combined.
f) Season with salt and pepper to taste.
g) Refrigerate for at least 1 hour before serving.

FISH AND SEAFOOD PASTA SALAD

25. Tuna and Artichoke Pasta Salad

INGREDIENTS:
- 2 cups fusilli pasta, cooked and cooled
- 1 can (6 oz) tuna, drained and flaked
- 1 cup cherry tomatoes, halved
- 1/2 cup marinated artichoke hearts, chopped
- 1/4 cup black olives, sliced
- 2 tablespoons capers
- 1/4 cup red onion, finely chopped
- 2 tablespoons fresh parsley, chopped
- 3 tablespoons olive oil
- 2 tablespoons red wine vinegar
- Salt and pepper to taste

INSTRUCTIONS:
a) In a large bowl, combine pasta, tuna, cherry tomatoes, artichoke hearts, olives, capers, red onion, and parsley.
b) In a small bowl, whisk together olive oil, red wine vinegar, salt, and pepper.
c) Pour the dressing over the pasta mixture and toss until well combined.
d) Refrigerate for at least 1 hour before serving.

26. Shrimp and Avocado Pasta Salad

INGREDIENTS:
- 2 cups penne pasta, cooked and cooled
- 1 lb cooked shrimp, peeled and deveined
- 2 avocados, diced
- 1 cup cherry tomatoes, halved
- 1/4 cup red onion, finely chopped
- 1/4 cup fresh cilantro, chopped
- Juice of 2 limes
- 3 tablespoons olive oil
- Salt and pepper to taste

INSTRUCTIONS:
a) In a large bowl, combine pasta, shrimp, avocados, cherry tomatoes, red onion, and cilantro.
b) Drizzle with lime juice and olive oil, then season with salt and pepper.
c) Toss until well combined.
d) Refrigerate for at least 1 hour before serving.

27. Smoked Salmon and Dill Pasta Salad

INGREDIENTS:
- 2 cups rotini pasta, cooked and cooled
- 4 oz smoked salmon, chopped
- 1/2 cup cucumber, diced
- 1/4 cup red onion, finely chopped
- 2 tablespoons capers
- 1/4 cup fresh dill, chopped
- 1/3 cup plain Greek yogurt
- Juice of 1 lemon
- Salt and pepper to taste

INSTRUCTIONS:
a) In a large bowl, combine pasta, smoked salmon, cucumber, red onion, capers, and dill.
b) In a small bowl, mix together Greek yogurt and lemon juice.
c) Pour the yogurt mixture over the pasta and toss until well coated.
d) Season with salt and pepper to taste.
e) Refrigerate for at least 1 hour before serving.

28. Crab and Mango Pasta Salad

INGREDIENTS:
- 2 cups farfalle pasta, cooked and cooled
- 1 lb lump crabmeat, picked over
- 1 mango, diced
- 1/2 cup red bell pepper, diced
- 1/4 cup red onion, finely chopped
- 1/4 cup fresh cilantro, chopped
- Juice of 2 limes
- 3 tablespoons mayonnaise
- Salt and pepper to taste

INSTRUCTIONS:
a) In a large bowl, combine pasta, lump crabmeat, mango, red bell pepper, red onion, and cilantro.
b) In a small bowl, whisk together lime juice and mayonnaise.
c) Pour the dressing over the pasta mixture and toss until well combined.
d) Season with salt and pepper to taste.
e) Refrigerate for at least 1 hour before serving.

29. Scallop and Asparagus Pasta Salad

INGREDIENTS:
- 2 cups gemelli pasta, cooked and cooled
- 1 lb scallops, seared
- 1 cup asparagus, blanched and chopped
- 1/4 cup sun-dried tomatoes, chopped
- 2 tablespoons pine nuts, toasted
- 1/4 cup fresh basil, chopped
- 3 tablespoons extra-virgin olive oil
- Juice of 1 lemon
- Salt and pepper to taste

INSTRUCTIONS:
a) In a large bowl, combine pasta, seared scallops, asparagus, sun-dried tomatoes, pine nuts, and basil.
b) In a small bowl, whisk together olive oil and lemon juice.
c) Pour the dressing over the pasta mixture and toss until well combined.
d) Season with salt and pepper to taste.
e) Refrigerate for at least 1 hour before serving.

30. Lemon Garlic Shrimp and Orzo Salad

INGREDIENTS:
- 2 cups orzo pasta, cooked and cooled
- 1 lb large shrimp, cooked and peeled
- 1 cup cherry tomatoes, halved
- 1/2 cup Kalamata olives, sliced
- 1/4 cup red onion, finely chopped
- 2 tablespoons fresh parsley, chopped
- Zest and juice of 2 lemons
- 3 tablespoons extra-virgin olive oil
- Salt and pepper to taste

INSTRUCTIONS:
a) In a large bowl, combine orzo pasta, cooked shrimp, cherry tomatoes, Kalamata olives, red onion, and parsley.
b) In a small bowl, whisk together lemon zest, lemon juice, olive oil, salt, and pepper.
c) Pour the dressing over the pasta mixture and toss until well coated.
d) Refrigerate for at least 1 hour before serving.

31. Grilled Tuna and White Bean Pasta Salad

INGREDIENTS:
- 2 cups rotini or Fusilli pasta, cooked and cooled
- 1 can (15 oz) white beans, drained and rinsed
- 1/2 cup cherry tomatoes, halved
- 1/4 cup red onion, finely chopped
- 1/4 cup Kalamata olives, sliced
- 1/4 cup fresh basil, chopped
- 2 cans (5 oz each) tuna, drained and flaked
- 3 tablespoons red wine vinegar
- 2 tablespoons extra-virgin olive oil
- Salt and pepper to taste

INSTRUCTIONS:
a) In a large bowl, combine pasta, white beans, cherry tomatoes, red onion, olives, basil, and tuna.
b) In a small bowl, whisk together red wine vinegar, olive oil, salt, and pepper.
c) Pour the dressing over the pasta mixture and toss until well combined.
d) Refrigerate for at least 1 hour before serving.

32. Cilantro Lime Salmon Pasta Salad

INGREDIENTS:
- 2 cups bowtie pasta, cooked and cooled
- 1 lb salmon fillet, grilled and flaked
- 1 cup corn kernels, cooked (fresh or frozen)
- 1/2 cup red bell pepper, diced
- 1/4 cup red onion, finely chopped
- 1/4 cup fresh cilantro, chopped
- Juice of 2 limes
- 3 tablespoons mayonnaise
- Salt and pepper to taste

INSTRUCTIONS:
a) In a large bowl, combine pasta, grilled salmon, corn, red bell pepper, red onion, and cilantro.
b) In a small bowl, whisk together lime juice and mayonnaise.
c) Pour the dressing over the pasta mixture and toss until well combined.
d) Season with salt and pepper to taste.
e) Refrigerate for at least 1 hour before serving.

33. Lobster and Mango Pasta Salad

INGREDIENTS:
- 2 cups penne pasta, cooked and cooled
- 1 lb lobster meat, cooked and chopped
- 1 mango, diced
- 1/2 cup cucumber, diced
- 1/4 cup red onion, finely chopped
- 1/4 cup fresh mint, chopped
- Juice of 2 limes
- 3 tablespoons extra-virgin olive oil
- Salt and pepper to taste

INSTRUCTIONS:
a) In a large bowl, combine pasta, lobster meat, mango, cucumber, red onion, and mint.
b) In a small bowl, whisk together lime juice, olive oil, salt, and pepper.
c) Pour the dressing over the pasta mixture and toss until well combined.
d) Refrigerate for at least 1 hour before serving.

34. Mediterranean Tzatziki Shrimp Pasta Salad

INGREDIENTS:
- 2 cups fusilli pasta, cooked and cooled
- 1 lb cooked shrimp, peeled and deveined
- 1 cup cherry tomatoes, halved
- 1/2 cup cucumber, diced
- 1/4 cup red onion, finely chopped
- 1/3 cup Kalamata olives, sliced
- 1/2 cup crumbled feta cheese
- 1/2 cup tzatziki sauce
- Fresh dill for garnish
- Salt and pepper to taste

INSTRUCTIONS:
a) In a large bowl, combine pasta, cooked shrimp, cherry tomatoes, cucumber, red onion, olives, and feta cheese.
b) Add tzatziki sauce and toss until well mixed.
c) Season with salt and pepper to taste.
d) Garnish with fresh dill.
e) Refrigerate for at least 1 hour before serving.

35. Shrimp and Cherry Tomato Pasta Salad

INGREDIENTS:
- ¾ Pounds shrimp, boiled until pink, about 2 minutes, and drained
- 12 ounces of rotini pasta

VEGETABLES
- 1 zucchini, chopped
- 2 yellow bell peppers, quartered
- 10 grape tomatoes, halved
- ½ teaspoon salt
- ½ white onion, sliced thin
- ¼ cup Black olives, sliced
- 2 Cups Baby spinach

CREAMY SAUCE
- 4 tablespoons unsalted butter
- 4 tablespoons all-purpose flour
- ½ teaspoon salt
- 1 teaspoon garlic powder
- 1 teaspoon onion powder
- 4 tablespoons nutritional yeast
- 2 cups milk
- 2 tablespoon lemon juice

FOR SERVING
- Black pepper

INSTRUCTIONS
PASTA:
a) Prepare pasta al dente per the instructions on the box.
b) Drain, and then place aside.

VEGETABLES:
c) Place a pan over moderate heat and add a little oil.
d) While stirring occasionally, cook the zucchini, bell peppers, onion, and salt for 8 minutes.
e) Add the tomatoes and cook for a further 3 minutes, or until the vegetables are tender.
f) Add the spinach and cook for about 3 minutes or until it is wilted.

CREAMY SAUCE:
g) In a pot over moderate heat, melt the butter.
h) Add the flour and gently whisk to create a smooth paste.
i) Add the milk and whisk again.

j) Whisk in the remaining sauce ingredients and simmer for about 5 minutes.

TO ASSEMBLE:

k) Combine cooked shrimp, cooked pasta, vegetables, black olives, and creamy sauce in a serving bowl.
l) Garnish with a sprinkle of cracked black pepper.

36. Nutty Tuna and Pasta Salad

INGREDIENTS:
- 1 head broccoli, separated into florets
- 8 large black olives, sliced
- 1 lb. penne pasta
- 1/2 cup walnut pieces, toasted
- 1 lb. fresh tuna steaks
- 4 cloves garlic, minced
- 1/4 cup water
- 2 tablespoons chopped fresh parsley
- 2 tablespoons fresh lemon juice
- 4 anchovy fillets, rinsed
- 1/4 cup white wine
- 3/4 cup olive oil
- 4 medium tomatoes, quartered
- 1 lb. mozzarella cheese, diced

INSTRUCTIONS:
a) Cook the pasta according to the instructions on the package.
b) Bring a salted pot of water to a boil. Cook in it the broccoli for 5 minutes. Remove it from the water and place it aside.
c) Place a large pan over medium heat. Stir in it the tuna in a with water, white wine, and lemon juice. put on the lid and cook them until the salmon is done for about 8 to 12 minutes.
d) Bread the salmon fillets into chunks.
e) Get a large mixing bowl: Toss in it the cooked salmon fish with broccoli, penne, fish, tomatoes, cheese, olives, walnuts, garlic, and parsley. Mix them well.
f) Place a large skillet over medium heat. Heat the oil in it. Slice the anchovies into small pieces. Cook them in the heated skillet until they melt in the oil.
g) Stir the mix into the pasta salad and mix them well. Serve your pasta salad right away.

POULTRY PASTA SALAD

37. Chicken Tenders & Farfalle Salad

INGREDIENTS:
- 6 eggs
- 3 green onions, thinly sliced
- 1 (16 oz.) package farfalle (bow tie) pasta
- 1/2 red onion, chopped
- 1/2 (16 oz.) bottle Italian-style salad dressing
- 6 chicken tenders
- 1 cucumber, sliced
- 4 romaine lettuce hearts, thinly sliced
- 1 bunch radishes, trimmed and sliced
- 2 carrots, peeled and sliced

INSTRUCTIONS:
a) Place the eggs in a large saucepan and cover them with water. Cook the eggs over medium heat until they start boiling.
b) Turn off the heat and let the eggs sit for 16 minutes. Rinse the eggs with some cold water to make them lose heat.
c) Peel the eggs and slice them then place them aside.
d) Place the chicken tenders in a large saucepan. Cover them with 1/4 cup of water. Cook them over medium heat until the chicken is done.
e) Drain the chicken tenders and cut them into small pieces.
f) Get a large mixing bowl: Toss in it the pasta, chicken, eggs, cucumber, radishes, carrots, green onions, and red onion. Add the Italian dressing and mix them again.
g) Place the salad in the fridge for 1 h 15 minutes.
h) Place lettuce hearts in serving plates. Divide the salad between them. Serve them right away.
i) Enjoy.

38. Creamy Penn Pasta Salad

INGREDIENTS:
- 1 (16 oz.) box mini penne pasta
- 1/3 cup chopped red onion
- 1 1/2 lb. chopped cooked chicken
- 1/2 (8 oz.) bottle creamy Caesar salad dressing
- 1/2 cup diced green bell pepper
- 2 hard-boiled eggs, chopped
- 1/3 cup grated Parmesan cheese

INSTRUCTIONS:
a) Cook the pasta according to the instructions on the package.
b) Get a large mixing bowl: Toss in it the pasta, chicken, green bell pepper, eggs, Parmesan cheese, and red onion.
c) Add the dressing and stir them well. Cover the bowl and place it in the fridge for 2 h 15
d) minutes. Adjust the seasoning of the salad and serve it.
e) Enjoy.

39. Feta and Roasted Turkey Salad

INGREDIENTS:

- 1 1/2 cup olive oil
- 3 cup cooked penne pasta
- 1/2 cup red wine vinegar
- 1 pint grape tomatoes, halved
- 1 tablespoons minced fresh garlic
- 8 oz. crumbled feta cheese
- 2 teaspoons dried oregano leaves
- 1 (5 oz.) package spring lettuce mix
- 3 cup Oven Roasted Turkey Breast, sliced thick and cubed
- 1/2 cup chopped Italian parsley
- 1/2 cup thinly sliced red onions
- 1 (16 oz.) jar pitted Kalamata olives, drained, chopped

INSTRUCTIONS:

a) Get a small mixing bowl: Combine in it the olive oil, vinegar, garlic and oregano. Mix them well to make the vinaigrette.
b) Get a large mixing bowl: Toss in it the rest of ingredients. Add the dressing and mix them again. Adjust the seasoning of the salad then serve it.
c) Enjoy.

40. Nutty Chicken Pasta Salad

INGREDIENTS:

- 6 slices bacon
- 1 (6 oz.) jar marinated artichoke hearts, drained 10 asparagus spears, ends trimmed and coarsely chopped
- 1/2 (16 oz.) package rotini, elbow, or penne 1 cooked chicken breast, cubed pasta
- 1/4 cup dried cranberries
- 3 tablespoons low fat mayonnaise
- 1/4 cup toasted sliced almonds
- 3 tablespoons balsamic vinaigrette salad dressing
- salt and pepper to taste
- 2 teaspoons lemon juice
- 1 teaspoons Worcestershire sauce

INSTRUCTIONS:

a) Place a large pan over medium heat. Cook in it the bacon until it becomes crisp. Remove it from the excess grease. Crumble it and place it aside.
b) Cook the pasta according to the instructions on the package.
c) Get a small mixing bowl: Combine in it the mayo, balsamic vinaigrette, lemon juice, and Worcestershire sauce. Mix them well.
d) Get a large mixing bowl: Toss in it the pasta with dressing. Add the artichoke, chicken, cranberries, almonds, crumbled bacon, and asparagus, a pinch of salt and pepper.
e) Stir them well. Chill the salad in the fridge for 1 h 10 min then serve it.
f) Enjoy.

41. Chicken Caesar Pasta Salad

INGREDIENTS:
- 2 cups rotini pasta, cooked and cooled
- 1 lb grilled chicken breast, sliced
- 1 cup cherry tomatoes, halved
- 1/2 cup black olives, sliced
- 1/4 cup grated Parmesan cheese
- 1/4 cup croutons
- 1/2 cup Caesar dressing
- Fresh parsley for garnish
- Salt and pepper to taste

INSTRUCTIONS:
a) In a large bowl, combine pasta, grilled chicken, cherry tomatoes, black olives, Parmesan cheese, and croutons.
b) Add Caesar dressing and toss until well mixed.
c) Garnish with fresh parsley.
d) Refrigerate for at least 1 hour before serving.

42. Turkey and Cranberry Pasta Salad

INGREDIENTS:
- 2 cups fusilli pasta, cooked and cooled
- 1 lb cooked turkey breast, diced
- 1/2 cup dried cranberries
- 1/4 cup red onion, finely chopped
- 1/2 cup celery, finely chopped
- 1/4 cup pecans, chopped
- 1/2 cup mayonnaise
- 2 tablespoons Dijon mustard
- Salt and pepper to taste

INSTRUCTIONS:
a) In a large bowl, combine pasta, diced turkey, dried cranberries, red onion, celery, and pecans.
b) In a small bowl, mix together mayonnaise, Dijon mustard, salt, and pepper.
c) Pour the dressing over the pasta mixture and toss until well coated.
d) Refrigerate for at least 1 hour before serving.

43. Lemon Herb Grilled Chicken Pasta Salad

INGREDIENTS:
- 2 cups penne pasta, cooked and cooled
- 1 lb grilled chicken breast, sliced
- 1 cup cherry tomatoes, halved
- 1/2 cup cucumber, diced
- 1/4 cup red onion, finely chopped
- 1/4 cup feta cheese, crumbled
- 2 tablespoons fresh parsley, chopped
- Juice of 2 lemons
- 3 tablespoons extra-virgin olive oil
- Salt and pepper to taste

INSTRUCTIONS:
a) In a large bowl, combine pasta, grilled chicken, cherry tomatoes, cucumber, red onion, feta cheese, and parsley.
b) In a small bowl, whisk together lemon juice, olive oil, salt, and pepper.
c) Pour the dressing over the pasta mixture and toss until well coated.
d) Refrigerate for at least 1 hour before serving.

44. Ranch Chicken and Bacon Pasta Salad

INGREDIENTS:
- 2 cups bowtie pasta, cooked and cooled
- 1 lb grilled chicken breast, diced
- 1/2 cup cherry tomatoes, halved
- 1/4 cup red onion, finely chopped
- 1/2 cup bacon, cooked and crumbled
- 1/4 cup shredded cheddar cheese
- 1/2 cup ranch dressing
- Chives for garnish
- Salt and pepper to taste

INSTRUCTIONS:
a) In a large bowl, combine pasta, diced grilled chicken, cherry tomatoes, red onion, bacon, and shredded cheddar cheese.
b) Add ranch dressing and toss until well mixed.
c) Garnish with chives.
d) Refrigerate for at least 1 hour before serving.

45. Curry Chicken and Mango Pasta Salad

INGREDIENTS:
- 2 cups large spiral pasta or farfalle pasta, cooked and cooled
- 1 lb cooked chicken breast, shredded
- 1 mango, diced
- 1/2 cup red bell pepper, diced
- 1/4 cup red onion, finely chopped
- 1/4 cup raisins
- 1/4 cup cashews, chopped
- 1/2 cup mayonnaise
- 1 tablespoon curry powder
- Salt and pepper to taste

INSTRUCTIONS:
a) In a large bowl, combine pasta, shredded chicken, mango, red bell pepper, red onion, raisins, and cashews.
b) In a small bowl, mix together mayonnaise and curry powder.
c) Pour the dressing over the pasta mixture and toss until well coated.
d) Season with salt and pepper to taste.
e) Refrigerate for at least 1 hour before serving.

46. Greek Chicken and Orzo Salad

INGREDIENTS:
- 2 cups orzo pasta, cooked and cooled
- 1 lb grilled chicken breast, diced
- 1 cup cherry tomatoes, halved
- 1/2 cup cucumber, diced
- 1/4 cup red onion, finely chopped
- 1/3 cup Kalamata olives, sliced
- 1/2 cup crumbled feta cheese
- 1/4 cup fresh parsley, chopped
- 3 tablespoons Greek dressing
- Salt and pepper to taste

INSTRUCTIONS:
a) In a large bowl, combine orzo pasta, grilled chicken, cherry tomatoes, cucumber, red onion, Kalamata olives, feta cheese, and parsley.
b) Add Greek dressing and toss until well mixed.
c) Season with salt and pepper to taste.
d) Refrigerate for at least 1 hour before serving.

47. Chicken and Black Bean Pasta Salad

INGREDIENTS:
- 2 cups rotini pasta, cooked and cooled
- 1 lb grilled chicken breast, sliced
- 1 can (15 oz) black beans, rinsed and drained
- 1 cup corn kernels, cooked (fresh or frozen)
- 1/2 cup red bell pepper, diced
- 1/4 cup red onion, finely chopped
- 1/4 cup fresh cilantro, chopped
- Juice of 2 limes
- 3 tablespoons olive oil
- 1 teaspoon cumin
- Salt and pepper to taste

INSTRUCTIONS:
a) In a large bowl, combine pasta, grilled chicken, black beans, corn, red bell pepper, red onion, and cilantro.
b) In a small bowl, whisk together lime juice, olive oil, cumin, salt, and pepper.
c) Pour the dressing over the pasta mixture and toss until well combined.
d) Refrigerate for at least 1 hour before serving.

48. Mango Curry Chicken Pasta Salad

INGREDIENTS:
- 2 cups penne pasta, cooked and cooled
- 1 lb cooked chicken breast, shredded
- 1 mango, diced
- 1/2 cup red bell pepper, diced
- 1/4 cup red onion, finely chopped
- 1/4 cup golden raisins
- 1/4 cup cashews, chopped
- 1/2 cup mayonnaise
- 1 tablespoon curry powder
- Salt and pepper to taste

INSTRUCTIONS:
a) In a large bowl, combine pasta, shredded chicken, mango, red bell pepper, red onion, raisins, and cashews.
b) In a small bowl, mix together mayonnaise and curry powder.
c) Pour the dressing over the pasta mixture and toss until well coated.
d) Season with salt and pepper to taste.
e) Refrigerate for at least 1 hour before serving.

49. Caprese Chicken Pesto Pasta Salad

INGREDIENTS:
- 2 cups farfalle pasta, cooked and cooled
- 1 lb grilled chicken breast, sliced
- 1 cup cherry tomatoes, halved
- 1/2 cup fresh mozzarella balls
- 1/4 cup fresh basil, chopped
- 2 tablespoons pine nuts, toasted
- 1/3 cup basil pesto
- 3 tablespoons balsamic glaze
- Salt and pepper to taste

INSTRUCTIONS:
a) In a large bowl, combine pasta, grilled chicken, cherry tomatoes, mozzarella balls, basil, and pine nuts.
b) Add basil pesto and toss until well coated.
c) Drizzle with balsamic glaze and season with salt and pepper to taste.
d) Refrigerate for at least 1 hour before serving.

50. Asian Sesame Chicken Noodle Salad

INGREDIENTS:
- 2 cups soba noodles, cooked and cooled
- 1 lb grilled chicken breast, shredded
- 1 cup shredded cabbage
- 1/2 cup shredded carrots
- 1/4 cup red bell pepper, thinly sliced
- 1/4 cup green onions, chopped
- 2 tablespoons sesame seeds, toasted
- 1/3 cup soy sauce
- 2 tablespoons sesame oil
- 1 tablespoon rice vinegar
- 1 tablespoon honey

INSTRUCTIONS:
a) In a large bowl, combine soba noodles, shredded chicken, cabbage, carrots, red bell pepper, green onions, and sesame seeds.
b) In a small bowl, whisk together soy sauce, sesame oil, rice vinegar, and honey.
c) Pour the dressing over the noodle mixture and toss until well coated.
d) Refrigerate for at least 1 hour before serving.

51. Lemon Herb Turkey and Asparagus Pasta Salad

INGREDIENTS:
- 2 cups fusilli pasta, cooked and cooled
- 1 lb cooked turkey breast, diced
- 1 cup asparagus, blanched and chopped
- 1/2 cup cherry tomatoes, halved
- 1/4 cup red onion, finely chopped
- 1/4 cup feta cheese, crumbled
- Zest and juice of 2 lemons
- 3 tablespoons extra-virgin olive oil
- 2 tablespoons fresh parsley, chopped
- Salt and pepper to taste

INSTRUCTIONS:
a) In a large bowl, combine pasta, diced turkey, asparagus, cherry tomatoes, red onion, and feta cheese.
b) In a small bowl, whisk together lemon zest, lemon juice, olive oil, salt, and pepper.
c) Pour the dressing over the pasta mixture and toss until well coated.
d) Garnish with fresh parsley.
e) Refrigerate for at least 1 hour before serving.

52. Chicken and Broccoli Pesto Pasta Salad

INGREDIENTS:
- 2 cups penne pasta, cooked and cooled
- 1 lb grilled chicken breast, sliced
- 1 cup broccoli florets, blanched
- 1/4 cup sun-dried tomatoes, chopped
- 1/4 cup pine nuts, toasted
- 1/2 cup Parmesan cheese, grated
- 1/3 cup basil pesto
- 3 tablespoons extra-virgin olive oil
- Salt and pepper to taste

INSTRUCTIONS:
a) In a large bowl, combine pasta, grilled chicken, broccoli, sun-dried tomatoes, pine nuts, and Parmesan cheese.
b) Add basil pesto and olive oil, tossing until well combined.
c) Season with salt and pepper to taste.
d) Refrigerate for at least 1 hour before serving.

53. Buffalo Chicken Pasta Salad

INGREDIENTS:
- 2 cups rotini pasta, cooked and cooled
- 1 lb cooked chicken breast, shredded
- 1/2 cup celery, finely chopped
- 1/4 cup red onion, finely chopped
- 1/4 cup blue cheese crumbles
- 1/3 cup buffalo sauce
- 1/4 cup ranch dressing
- Fresh chives for garnish
- Salt and pepper to taste

INSTRUCTIONS:
a) In a large bowl, combine pasta, shredded chicken, celery, red onion, and blue cheese crumbles.
b) In a small bowl, whisk together buffalo sauce and ranch dressing.
c) Pour the dressing over the pasta mixture and toss until well coated.
d) Garnish with fresh chives.
e) Refrigerate for at least 1 hour before serving.

54. Cranberry Walnut Chicken Pasta Salad

INGREDIENTS:
- 2 cups farfalle pasta, cooked and cooled
- 1 lb cooked chicken breast, diced
- 1/2 cup dried cranberries
- 1/4 cup walnuts, chopped and toasted
- 1/2 cup celery, finely chopped
- 1/4 cup red onion, finely chopped
- 1/2 cup mayonnaise
- 2 tablespoons Dijon mustard
- Salt and pepper to taste

INSTRUCTIONS:
a) In a large bowl, combine pasta, diced chicken, dried cranberries, walnuts, celery, and red onion.
b) In a small bowl, mix together mayonnaise, Dijon mustard, salt, and pepper.
c) Pour the dressing over the pasta mixture and toss until well coated.
d) Refrigerate for at least 1 hour before serving.

COLD MEATS PASTA SALAD

55.Italian Cold Pasta Salad with Salami

INGREDIENTS:
- 2 cups rotini pasta, cooked and cooled
- 1/2 lb salami, sliced and cut into bite-sized pieces
- 1 cup cherry tomatoes, halved
- 1/2 cup mozzarella balls (bocconcini)
- 1/4 cup black olives, sliced
- 1/4 cup red onion, finely chopped
- 1/4 cup fresh basil, chopped
- 3 tablespoons extra-virgin olive oil
- 2 tablespoons red wine vinegar
- Salt and pepper to taste

INSTRUCTIONS:

a) In a large bowl, combine pasta, salami, cherry tomatoes, mozzarella balls, black olives, red onion, and fresh basil.
b) In a small bowl, whisk together olive oil, red wine vinegar, salt, and pepper.
c) Pour the dressing over the pasta mixture and toss until well coated.
d) Refrigerate for at least 1 hour before serving.

56. Turkey and Cranberry Cold Pasta Salad

INGREDIENTS:
- 2 cups fusilli or farfalle pasta, cooked and cooled
- 1/2 lb turkey breast, cooked and diced
- 1/2 cup dried cranberries
- 1/4 cup pecans, chopped and toasted
- 1/2 cup celery, finely chopped
- 1/4 cup red onion, finely chopped
- 1/3 cup mayonnaise
- 2 tablespoons Dijon mustard
- Salt and pepper to taste

INSTRUCTIONS:
a) In a large bowl, combine pasta, diced turkey, dried cranberries, pecans, celery, and red onion.
b) In a small bowl, mix together mayonnaise, Dijon mustard, salt, and pepper.
c) Pour the dressing over the pasta mixture and toss until well coated.
d) Refrigerate for at least 1 hour before serving.

57. Cold Pasta Salad with Ham and Cheddar

INGREDIENTS:
- 2 cups elbow macaroni, cooked and cooled
- 1/2 lb ham, diced
- 1 cup cheddar cheese, cubed
- 1/2 cup cherry tomatoes, halved
- 1/4 cup red bell pepper, diced
- 1/4 cup green onions, chopped
- 1/3 cup mayonnaise
- 2 tablespoons sour cream
- 1 tablespoon Dijon mustard
- Salt and pepper to taste

INSTRUCTIONS:
a) In a large bowl, combine pasta, diced ham, cheddar cheese, cherry tomatoes, red bell pepper, and green onions.
b) In a small bowl, whisk together mayonnaise, sour cream, Dijon mustard, salt, and pepper.
c) Pour the dressing over the pasta mixture and toss until well coated.
d) Refrigerate for at least 1 hour before serving.

58. Chicken Caesar Cold Pasta Salad

INGREDIENTS:
- 2 cups penne pasta, cooked and cooled
- 1 lb grilled chicken breast, sliced
- 1/2 cup cherry tomatoes, halved
- 1/4 cup black olives, sliced
- 1/4 cup grated Parmesan cheese
- 1/4 cup croutons, crushed
- 1/2 cup Caesar dressing
- Fresh parsley for garnish
- Salt and pepper to taste

INSTRUCTIONS:
a) In a large bowl, combine pasta, grilled chicken, cherry tomatoes, black olives, Parmesan cheese, and crushed croutons.
b) Add Caesar dressing and toss until well mixed.
c) Garnish with fresh parsley.
d) Refrigerate for at least 1 hour before serving.

59. Greek Orzo Pasta Salad with Gyro Meat

INGREDIENTS:
- 2 cups orzo pasta, cooked and cooled
- 1/2 lb gyro meat, sliced
- 1 cup cucumber, diced
- 1/2 cup cherry tomatoes, halved
- 1/4 cup red onion, finely chopped
- 1/3 cup Kalamata olives, sliced
- 1/2 cup feta cheese, crumbled
- 3 tablespoons Greek dressing
- Fresh oregano for garnish
- Salt and pepper to taste

INSTRUCTIONS:
a) In a large bowl, combine orzo pasta, sliced gyro meat, cucumber, cherry tomatoes, red onion, Kalamata olives, and feta cheese.
b) Add Greek dressing and toss until well mixed.
c) Garnish with fresh oregano.
d) Refrigerate for at least 1 hour before serving.

60. Roast Beef and Cheddar Pasta Salad

INGREDIENTS:
- 2 cups fusilli pasta, cooked and cooled
- 1/2 lb roast beef, thinly sliced and cut into strips
- 1/2 cup cheddar cheese, cubed
- 1/4 cup red bell pepper, diced
- 1/4 cup green bell pepper, diced
- 1/4 cup red onion, finely chopped
- 1/3 cup creamy horseradish dressing
- Salt and pepper to taste

INSTRUCTIONS:
a) In a large bowl, combine pasta, roast beef, cheddar cheese, red bell pepper, green bell pepper, and red onion.
b) Add creamy horseradish dressing and toss until well coated.
c) Season with salt and pepper to taste.
d) Refrigerate for at least 1 hour before serving.

61. Bacon Ranch Cold Chicken Pasta Salad

INGREDIENTS:
- 2 cups rotini pasta, cooked and cooled
- 1 lb cooked chicken breast, diced
- 1/2 cup bacon, cooked and crumbled
- 1/2 cup cherry tomatoes, halved
- 1/4 cup red onion, finely chopped
- 1/2 cup cheddar cheese, shredded
- 1/3 cup ranch dressing
- Fresh chives for garnish
- Salt and pepper to taste

INSTRUCTIONS:
a) In a large bowl, combine pasta, diced chicken, bacon, cherry tomatoes, red onion, and cheddar cheese.
b) Add ranch dressing and toss until well mixed.
c) Garnish with fresh chives.
d) Refrigerate for at least 1 hour before serving.

62.Italian Antipasto Pasta Salad

INGREDIENTS:
- 2 cups bowtie pasta, cooked and cooled
- 1/2 lb salami, sliced and cut into strips
- 1/2 cup provolone cheese, cubed
- 1/4 cup black olives, sliced
- 1/4 cup green olives, sliced
- 1/4 cup roasted red peppers, chopped
- 1/4 cup artichoke hearts, chopped
- 1/3 cup Italian dressing
- Fresh basil for garnish
- Salt and pepper to taste

INSTRUCTIONS:
a) In a large bowl, combine pasta, salami, provolone cheese, black olives, green olives, roasted red peppers, and artichoke hearts.
b) Add Italian dressing and toss until well coated.
c) Garnish with fresh basil.
d) Refrigerate for at least 1 hour before serving.

63. Smoked Turkey and Avocado Pasta Salad

INGREDIENTS:
- 2 cups penne pasta, cooked and cooled
- 1/2 lb smoked turkey, diced
- 1 avocado, diced
- 1/2 cup cherry tomatoes, halved
- 1/4 cup red onion, finely chopped
- 1/4 cup feta cheese, crumbled
- 2 tablespoons fresh cilantro, chopped
- Juice of 2 limes
- 3 tablespoons olive oil
- Salt and pepper to taste

INSTRUCTIONS:
a) In a large bowl, combine pasta, diced smoked turkey, diced avocado, cherry tomatoes, red onion, feta cheese, and cilantro.
b) Drizzle with lime juice and olive oil.
c) Toss until well combined.
d) Season with salt and pepper to taste.
e) Refrigerate for at least 1 hour before serving.

64. Grilled Sausage and Vegetable Pasta Salad

INGREDIENTS:
- 2 cups rotini pasta, cooked and cooled
- 1/2 lb grilled sausage, sliced
- 1 cup zucchini, diced
- 1 cup cherry tomatoes, halved
- 1/2 cup red bell pepper, diced
- 1/4 cup red onion, finely chopped
- 1/3 cup balsamic vinaigrette
- Fresh basil for garnish
- Salt and pepper to taste

INSTRUCTIONS:
a) In a large bowl, combine pasta, grilled sausage, zucchini, cherry tomatoes, red bell pepper, and red onion.
b) Add balsamic vinaigrette and toss until well coated.
c) Garnish with fresh basil.
d) Season with salt and pepper to taste.
e) Refrigerate for at least 1 hour before serving.

65. Shrimp and Avocado Cold Pasta Salad

INGREDIENTS:
- 2 cups rotini pasta, cooked and cooled
- 1/2 lb cooked shrimp, peeled and deveined
- 1 avocado, diced
- 1/2 cup cherry tomatoes, halved
- 1/4 cup red onion, finely chopped
- 1/4 cup cucumber, diced
- 2 tablespoons fresh cilantro, chopped
- Juice of 2 limes
- 3 tablespoons olive oil
- Salt and pepper to taste

INSTRUCTIONS:
a) In a large bowl, combine pasta, cooked shrimp, diced avocado, cherry tomatoes, red onion, cucumber, and cilantro.
b) Drizzle with lime juice and olive oil.
c) Toss until well combined.
d) Season with salt and pepper to taste.
e) Refrigerate for at least 1 hour before serving.

66. Pastrami and Swiss Cold Pasta Salad

INGREDIENTS:
- 2 cups penne pasta, cooked and cooled
- 1/2 lb pastrami, sliced and cut into strips
- 1/2 cup Swiss cheese, cubed
- 1/4 cup dill pickles, chopped
- 1/4 cup red onion, finely chopped
- 1/3 cup mayonnaise
- 2 tablespoons Dijon mustard
- Salt and pepper to taste

INSTRUCTIONS:
a) In a large bowl, combine pasta, pastrami, Swiss cheese, dill pickles, and red onion.
b) In a small bowl, mix together mayonnaise, Dijon mustard, salt, and pepper.
c) Pour the dressing over the pasta mixture and toss until well coated.
d) Refrigerate for at least 1 hour before serving.

67. Tuna and White Bean Cold Pasta Salad

INGREDIENTS:
- 2 cups fusilli pasta, cooked and cooled
- 1 can (15 oz) white beans, drained and rinsed
- 1 can (5 oz) tuna, drained and flaked
- 1/2 cup cherry tomatoes, halved
- 1/4 cup red onion, finely chopped
- 1/4 cup black olives, sliced
- 2 tablespoons fresh parsley, chopped
- 3 tablespoons red wine vinegar
- 2 tablespoons olive oil
- Salt and pepper to taste

INSTRUCTIONS:
a) In a large bowl, combine pasta, white beans, tuna, cherry tomatoes, red onion, black olives, and parsley.
b) In a small bowl, whisk together red wine vinegar, olive oil, salt, and pepper.
c) Pour the dressing over the pasta mixture and toss until well coated.
d) Refrigerate for at least 1 hour before serving.

68. BBQ Chicken and Corn Pasta Salad

INGREDIENTS:
- 2 cups bowtie pasta, cooked and cooled
- 1 lb grilled chicken breast, diced
- 1 cup corn kernels, cooked (fresh or frozen)
- 8 strips bacon cooked
- 1/4 cup red onion, finely chopped
- 1/4 cup cilantro, chopped
- 1/3 cup barbecue sauce
- 2 tablespoons mayonnaise
- Salt and pepper to taste

INSTRUCTIONS:
a) In a large bowl, combine pasta, diced grilled chicken, corn, bacon, red onion, and cilantro.
b) In a small bowl, mix together barbecue sauce and mayonnaise.
c) Pour the dressing over the pasta mixture and toss until well coated.
d) Season with salt and pepper to taste.
e) Refrigerate for at least 1 hour before serving.

69. Italian Sausage and Peppers Pasta Salad

INGREDIENTS:
- 2 cups rotini pasta, cooked and cooled
- 1/2 lb Italian sausage, grilled and sliced
- 1/2 cup bell peppers (assorted colors), sliced
- 1/4 cup red onion, finely chopped
- 1/4 cup black olives, sliced
- 1/3 cup Italian dressing
- Fresh basil for garnish
- Salt and pepper to taste

INSTRUCTIONS:
a) In a large bowl, combine pasta, grilled Italian sausage, bell peppers, red onion, and black olives.
b) Add Italian dressing and toss until well mixed.
c) Garnish with fresh basil.
d) Season with salt and pepper to taste.
e) Refrigerate for at least 1 hour before serving.

70. Copycat Ruby Tuesday Pasta Salad

INGREDIENTS:
- 10 ounces frozen peas
- 1 pound rotini noodles
- ¼ cup buttermilk
- 2 tablespoons ranch seasoning
- ½ teaspoon garlic salt
- ½ teaspoon black pepper
- Parmesan, to garnish
- 2 cups mayonnaise
- 8 ounces ham, diced

INSTRUCTIONS

PASTA SALAD
a) Prepare the rotini noodles following the instructions on the box.
b) To halt the cooking process, drain thoroughly and rinse with cold water.
c) After rinsing, make sure it drains very well.

DRESSING
d) Combine the mayonnaise, buttermilk, ranch seasoning, garlic salt, and black pepper.

TO ASSEMBLE
e) Combine the pasta, ham, and frozen peas in a serving dish.
f) Add the dressing and stir until it is evenly distributed.
g) Refrigerate for at least one hour to let the flavors meld.
h) Stir it thoroughly before serving it with grated parmesan on top.

VEGGIE PASTA SALAD

71. Vegan Rigatoni Basil Salad

INGREDIENTS:
- 1 1/2 (8 oz.) packages rigatoni pasta
- 6 leaves fresh basil, thinly sliced
- 2 tablespoons olive oil
- 6 sprigs fresh cilantro, minced
- 2 cloves garlic, minced
- 1/4 cup olive oil
- 1/2 (16 oz.) package tofu, drained and cubed
- 1/2 teaspoons dried thyme
- 1 1/2 teaspoons soy sauce
- 1 small onion, thinly sliced
- 1 large tomato, cubed
- 1 carrot, shredded

INSTRUCTIONS:
a) Cook the pasta according to the instructions on the package.
b) Place a large pan over medium heat. Heat 2 tablespoons of olive oil in it. Add the garlic and cook it for 1 min 30 sec.
c) Stir in the thyme with tofu. Cook them for 9 minutes. Stir in the soy sauce and turn off the heat.
d) Get a large mixing bowl: Toss in it the rigatoni, tofu mix, onion, tomato, carrot, basil, and cilantro. Drizzle the olive oil over the pasta salad then serve it.
e) Enjoy.

72. BLT Pasta Salad

INGREDIENTS:
- 2 cups elbow macaroni
- 1 ¼ cups mayonnaise
- 2 Tablespoons balsamic vinegar
- 1 cup halved cherry tomatoes
- ¼ cup chopped red bell pepper
- 3 Tablespoons chopped scallions
- ½ cup shredded Cheddar cheese
- Salt and pepper to taste
- ½ teaspoons dill
- 10 bacon slices
- 8 oz. chopped romaine lettuce

INSTRUCTIONS:
a) Cook the macaroni in a pot of salted water for 10 minutes. Drain and transfer to a salad bowl.
b) Add the mayonnaise, balsamic vinegar, tomatoes, bell pepper, scallions, cheese, salt, pepper, and dill to the macaroni and stir well to combine.
c) Chill for 3 hours.
d) Fry the bacon for 10 minutes, until crispy.
e) Drain the bacon and let cool, then crumble the bacon.
f) Top the salad with the crumbled bacon.
g) Serve on romaine lettuce.

73. Macaroni Coleslaw

INGREDIENTS:
- 1 package (7 ounces) ring macaroni or ditalini
- 1 package (14 ounces) coleslaw mix
- 2 medium onions, finely chopped
- 2 celery ribs, finely chopped
- 1 medium cucumber, finely chopped
- 1 medium green pepper, finely chopped
- 1 can (8 ounces) whole water chestnuts, drained and chopped

DRESSING:
- 1-1/2 cups Miracle Whip Light
- 1/3 cup sugar
- 1/4 cup cider vinegar
- 1/2 teaspoon salt
- 1/4 teaspoon pepper

INSTRUCTIONS:
a) Cook the macaroni according to package directions; drain and rinse in cold water. Transfer to a large bowl.
b) Add the coleslaw mix, onions, celery, cucumber, green pepper, and water chestnuts to the bowl with macaroni.
c) In a small bowl, whisk together the dressing ingredients. Pour the dressing over the salad and toss to coat.
d) Cover and refrigerate for at least 1 hour before serving.

74. Kalamata Rotini Salad

INGREDIENTS:
- 1 (12 oz.) package tri-colored rotini pasta
- 4 Roma tomatoes, diced
- 1 (12 oz.) jar oil-packed sun-dried tomatoes, drained, cut into strips
- 1 small head broccoli, broken into small florets
- 1 small zucchini, chopped
- 1/2 teaspoons minced garlic
- 1 small cucumber, chopped
- 1 small red onion, diced
- 1 small yellow bell pepper, chopped
- 1 (12 oz.) jar marinated artichoke hearts, drained and chopped
- 2 ripe avocados
- 1 (16 oz.) bottle Greek vinaigrette salad dressing
- 1 (12 oz.) jar pitted Kalamata olives, sliced
- 1 (8 oz.) jar roasted red bell peppers, drained, cut into strips

INSTRUCTIONS:
a) Cook the pasta according to the instructions on the package.
b) Bring a large pot of water to a boil. Place a steamer on it. Cook in it the broccoli for 5 min with the lid on.
c) Clean the broccoli with some cool water and drain it. Chop it and place it aside. Get a large mixing bowl:
d) Combine in it the broccoli with pasta, garlic, red onion, artichoke hearts, Kalamata olives, roasted red peppers, Roma tomatoes, sun-dried tomatoes, zucchini, cucumber, and yellow pepper. Mix them well.
e) Get a small mixing bowl: Mash in it the avocado until it becomes smooth. Add the Greek dressing and mix them well until they become creamy to make the dressing.
f) Add the avocado dressing to the salad and toss it well. Adjust the seasoning of the salad and chill it in the fridge until ready to serve. Enjoy.

75. Tortellini Jarred Salad

INGREDIENTS:
- 1 (9 oz.) package spinach and cheese
- 1 canning jar tortellini
- salt and ground black pepper to taste
- 1 (4 oz.) jar pesto
- 1/4 cup halved, seeded, and sliced English cucumber
- 1/4 cup halved cherry tomatoes
- 1/4 cup matchstick-sized pieces red onion
- 1/2 cup chopped mache

INSTRUCTIONS:
a) Cook the pasta according to the instructions on the package.
b) Spread the pesto in the jar then top it with the cucumbers, tomatoes, onions, tortellini, and mache. Season them with some salt and pepper.
c) Serve your salad right away or refrigerate it until you are ready to serve it.

76. Garlic-Mushroom Fusilli with Pear Salad

INGREDIENTS:
- 1 brown onion
- 2 cloves of garlic
- 1 packet of sliced mushrooms
- 1 sachet of garlic & herb seasoning
- 1 packet of light cooking cream
- 1 sachet of chicken-style stock powder
- 1 packet of fusilli (Contains Gluten; May be present: Egg, Soy)
- 1 pear
- 1 bag of mixed salad leaves
- 1 packet of Parmesan cheese
- Olive oil
- 1.75 cups of boiling water
- A drizzle of vinegar (balsamic or white wine)

INSTRUCTIONS:

a) Boil the kettle. Finely chop the brown onion and garlic. Heat a large saucepan over medium-high heat with a generous drizzle of olive oil. Cook the sliced mushrooms and onion, stirring occasionally, until they are just softened, which takes about 6-8 minutes. Add the garlic and garlic & herb seasoning, and cook until fragrant for about 1 minute.

b) Add the light cooking cream, boiling water (1 3/4 cups for 2 people), chicken-style stock powder, and fusilli. Stir to combine and bring it to a boil. Reduce the heat to medium, cover with a lid, and cook, stirring occasionally, until the pasta is 'al dente,' which takes around 11 minutes. Stir through shaved Parmesan cheese and season to taste with salt and pepper.

c) While the pasta is cooking, thinly slice the pear. In a medium bowl, add a drizzle of vinegar and olive oil. Top the dressing with mixed salad leaves and pear. Season and toss to combine.

d) Divide the one-pot creamy mushroom fusilli between bowls. Serve with the pear salad. Enjoy your delicious meal!

77. Mediterranean Vegetable Pasta Salad

INGREDIENTS:
- 2 cups penne pasta, cooked and cooled
- 1 cup cherry tomatoes, halved
- 1 cucumber, diced
- 1/2 cup Kalamata olives, sliced
- 1/4 cup red onion, finely chopped
- 1/2 cup feta cheese, crumbled
- 1/3 cup extra-virgin olive oil
- 2 tablespoons red wine vinegar
- 1 teaspoon dried oregano
- Salt and pepper to taste

INSTRUCTIONS:
a) In a large bowl, combine pasta, cherry tomatoes, cucumber, Kalamata olives, red onion, and feta cheese.
b) In a small bowl, whisk together olive oil, red wine vinegar, dried oregano, salt, and pepper.
c) Pour the dressing over the pasta mixture and toss until well coated.
d) Refrigerate for at least 1 hour before serving.

78.Pesto Veggie Spiral Pasta Salad

INGREDIENTS:
- 2 cups spiral pasta, cooked and cooled
- 1 cup cherry tomatoes, halved
- 1/2 cup artichoke hearts, chopped
- 1/2 cup black olives, sliced
- 1/4 cup red onion, finely chopped
- 1/3 cup pesto sauce
- 3 tablespoons grated Parmesan cheese
- Salt and pepper to taste

INSTRUCTIONS:
a) In a large bowl, combine pasta, cherry tomatoes, artichoke hearts, black olives, and red onion.
b) Add pesto sauce and toss until well mixed.
c) Sprinkle grated Parmesan cheese over the salad.
d) Season with salt and pepper to taste.
e) Refrigerate for at least 1 hour before serving.

79. Rainbow Veggie Pasta Salad

INGREDIENTS:
- 2 cups bowtie pasta, cooked and cooled
- 1 cup broccoli florets, blanched
- 1 cup bell peppers (assorted colors), diced
- 1/2 cup cherry tomatoes, halved
- 1/4 cup red onion, finely chopped
- 1/3 cup Italian dressing
- Fresh basil for garnish
- Salt and pepper to taste

INSTRUCTIONS:
a) In a large bowl, combine pasta, broccoli florets, bell peppers, cherry tomatoes, and red onion.
b) Add Italian dressing and toss until well coated.
c) Garnish with fresh basil.
d) Season with salt and pepper to taste.
e) Refrigerate for at least 1 hour before serving.

80. Asian Sesame Vegetable Noodle Salad

INGREDIENTS:
- 2 cups soba noodles, cooked and cooled
- 1 cup snow peas, blanched and sliced
- 1 cup shredded carrots
- 1/2 cup red bell pepper, thinly sliced
- 1/4 cup green onions, chopped
- 2 tablespoons sesame seeds, toasted
- 1/3 cup soy sauce
- 2 tablespoons rice vinegar
- 1 tablespoon sesame oil
- 1 tablespoon honey

INSTRUCTIONS:
a) In a large bowl, combine soba noodles, snow peas, shredded carrots, red bell pepper, green onions, and sesame seeds.
b) In a small bowl, whisk together soy sauce, rice vinegar, sesame oil, and honey.
c) Pour the dressing over the noodle mixture and toss until well coated.
d) Refrigerate for at least 1 hour before serving.

81. Caprese Vegetable Pasta Salad

INGREDIENTS:
- 2 cups farfalle pasta, cooked and cooled
- 1 cup cherry tomatoes, halved
- 1 cup fresh mozzarella balls
- 1/4 cup fresh basil, chopped
- 2 tablespoons pine nuts, toasted
- 3 tablespoons balsamic glaze
- 3 tablespoons extra-virgin olive oil
- Salt and pepper to taste

INSTRUCTIONS:
a) In a large bowl, combine pasta, cherry tomatoes, mozzarella balls, basil, and pine nuts.
b) Drizzle with balsamic glaze and olive oil.
c) Toss until well combined.
d) Season with salt and pepper to taste.
e) Refrigerate for at least 1 hour before serving.

82. Greek Orzo Vegetable Salad

INGREDIENTS:
- 2 cups orzo pasta, cooked and cooled
- 1 cup cucumber, diced
- 1 cup cherry tomatoes, halved
- 1/2 cup Kalamata olives, sliced
- 1/4 cup red onion, finely chopped
- 1/2 cup feta cheese, crumbled
- 3 tablespoons Greek dressing
- Fresh oregano for garnish
- Salt and pepper to taste

INSTRUCTIONS:
a) In a large bowl, combine orzo pasta, cucumber, cherry tomatoes, Kalamata olives, red onion, and feta cheese.
b) Add Greek dressing and toss until well mixed.
c) Garnish with fresh oregano.
d) Season with salt and pepper to taste.
e) Refrigerate for at least 1 hour before serving.

83. Roasted Vegetable and Chickpea Pasta Salad

INGREDIENTS:
- 2 cups fusilli pasta, cooked and cooled
- 1 cup cherry tomatoes, halved
- 1 cup zucchini, diced
- 1 cup bell peppers (assorted colors), diced
- 1/2 cup red onion, finely chopped
- 1 can (15 oz) chickpeas, drained and rinsed
- 3 tablespoons balsamic vinaigrette
- 3 tablespoons olive oil
- 2 tablespoons fresh basil, chopped
- Salt and pepper to taste

INSTRUCTIONS:
a) In a large bowl, combine pasta, cherry tomatoes, zucchini, bell peppers, red onion, and chickpeas.
b) In a small bowl, whisk together balsamic vinaigrette, olive oil, basil, salt, and pepper.
c) Pour the dressing over the pasta mixture and toss until well coated.
d) Refrigerate for at least 1 hour before serving.

84. Spinach and Artichoke Cold Pasta Salad

INGREDIENTS:
- 2 cups rotini pasta, cooked and cooled
- 1 cup baby spinach leaves
- 1 cup artichoke hearts, chopped
- 1/2 cup cherry tomatoes, halved
- 1/4 cup red onion, finely chopped
- 1/3 cup Greek yogurt
- 2 tablespoons mayonnaise
- 2 tablespoons grated Parmesan cheese
- 1 tablespoon lemon juice
- Salt and pepper to taste

INSTRUCTIONS:
a) In a large bowl, combine pasta, baby spinach, artichoke hearts, cherry tomatoes, and red onion.
b) In a small bowl, mix together Greek yogurt, mayonnaise, Parmesan cheese, lemon juice, salt, and pepper.
c) Pour the dressing over the pasta mixture and toss until well coated.
d) Refrigerate for at least 1 hour before serving.

85. Thai Peanut Vegetable Noodle Salad

INGREDIENTS:
- 2 cups rice noodles, cooked and cooled
- 1 cup broccoli florets, blanched
- 1 cup shredded carrots
- 1/2 cup red bell pepper, thinly sliced
- 1/4 cup green onions, chopped
- 1/4 cup peanuts, chopped
- 1/3 cup peanut sauce
- 2 tablespoons soy sauce
- 1 tablespoon lime juice
- 1 tablespoon honey

INSTRUCTIONS:
a) In a large bowl, combine rice noodles, broccoli florets, shredded carrots, red bell pepper, green onions, and peanuts.
b) In a small bowl, whisk together peanut sauce, soy sauce, lime juice, and honey.
c) Pour the dressing over the noodle mixture and toss until well coated.
d) Refrigerate for at least 1 hour before serving.

86. Caesar Veggie Pasta Salad

INGREDIENTS:
- 2 cups bowtie pasta, cooked and cooled
- 1 cup cherry tomatoes, halved
- 1 cup cucumber, diced
- 1/2 cup black olives, sliced
- 1/4 cup red onion, finely chopped
- 1/4 cup grated Parmesan cheese
- 1/4 cup croutons, crushed
- 1/2 cup Caesar dressing
- Fresh parsley for garnish
- Salt and pepper to taste

INSTRUCTIONS:
a) In a large bowl, combine pasta, cherry tomatoes, cucumber, black olives, red onion, Parmesan cheese, and crushed croutons.
b) Add Caesar dressing and toss until well mixed.
c) Garnish with fresh parsley.
d) Refrigerate for at least 1 hour before serving.

COLD FRUITY PASTA SALADS

87. Tropical Fruit and Shrimp Pasta Salad

INGREDIENTS:
- 2 cups fusilli pasta, cooked and cooled
- 1/2 lb cooked shrimp, peeled and deveined
- 1 cup pineapple chunks
- 1 cup mango, diced
- 1/2 cup red bell pepper, diced
- 1/4 cup red onion, finely chopped
- 1/3 cup coconut flakes
- 3 tablespoons lime juice
- 2 tablespoons honey
- Salt and pepper to taste

INSTRUCTIONS:
a) In a large bowl, combine pasta, cooked shrimp, pineapple chunks, mango, red bell pepper, red onion, and coconut flakes.
b) In a small bowl, whisk together lime juice and honey.
c) Pour the dressing over the pasta mixture and toss until well coated.
d) Season with salt and pepper to taste.
e) Refrigerate for at least 1 hour before serving.

88. Berry and Feta Pasta Salad

INGREDIENTS:
- 2 cups bowtie pasta, cooked and cooled
- 1 cup strawberries, sliced
- 1/2 cup blueberries
- 1/2 cup raspberries
- 1/2 cup feta cheese, crumbled
- 1/4 cup fresh mint, chopped
- 3 tablespoons balsamic glaze
- 3 tablespoons olive oil
- Salt and pepper to taste

INSTRUCTIONS:
a) In a large bowl, combine pasta, strawberries, blueberries, raspberries, feta cheese, and fresh mint.
b) Drizzle with balsamic glaze and olive oil.
c) Toss until well combined.
d) Season with salt and pepper to taste.
e) Refrigerate for at least 1 hour before serving.

89. Citrus and Avocado Pasta Salad

INGREDIENTS:
- 2 cups rotini pasta, cooked and cooled
- 1 orange, segmented
- 1 grapefruit, segmented
- 1 avocado, diced
- 1/4 cup red onion, finely chopped
- 2 tablespoons fresh cilantro, chopped
- 3 tablespoons orange juice
- 2 tablespoons lime juice
- 3 tablespoons olive oil
- Salt and pepper to taste

INSTRUCTIONS:
a) In a large bowl, combine pasta, orange segments, grapefruit segments, diced avocado, red onion, and cilantro.
b) In a small bowl, whisk together orange juice, lime juice, and olive oil.
c) Pour the dressing over the pasta mixture and toss until well coated.
d) Season with salt and pepper to taste.
e) Refrigerate for at least 1 hour before serving.

90. Watermelon and Feta Pasta Salad

INGREDIENTS:
- 2 cups penne or macaroni pasta, cooked and cooled
- 2 cups watermelon, diced
- 1/2 cup cucumber, diced
- 1/4 cup red onion, finely chopped
- 1/2 cup feta cheese, crumbled
- 2 tablespoons fresh mint, chopped
- 3 tablespoons balsamic glaze
- 3 tablespoons olive oil
- Salt and pepper to taste

INSTRUCTIONS:
a) In a large bowl, combine pasta, watermelon, cucumber, red onion, feta cheese, and fresh mint.
b) Drizzle with balsamic glaze and olive oil.
c) Toss until well combined.
d) Season with salt and pepper to taste.
e) Refrigerate for at least 1 hour before serving.

91. Mango and Black Bean Pasta Salad

INGREDIENTS:
- 2 cups farfalle pasta, cooked and cooled
- 1 mango, diced
- 1 cup black beans, rinsed and drained
- 1 cup corn roasted (optional)
- 1/2 cup red bell pepper, diced
- 1/4 cup red onion, finely chopped
- 2 tablespoons fresh cilantro, chopped
- 3 tablespoons lime juice
- 2 tablespoons olive oil
- 1 teaspoon cumin
- Salt and pepper to taste

INSTRUCTIONS:

a) In a large bowl, combine pasta, diced mango, black beans, corn, red bell pepper, red onion, and cilantro.

b) In a small bowl, whisk together lime juice, olive oil, cumin, salt, and pepper.

c) Pour the dressing over the pasta mixture and toss until well coated.

d) Refrigerate for at least 1 hour before serving.

92. Apple and Walnut Pasta Salad

INGREDIENTS:
- 2 cups penne pasta, cooked and cooled
- 2 apples, diced
- 1/2 cup celery, finely chopped
- 1/4 cup walnuts, chopped and toasted
- 1/4 cup raisins
- 1/3 cup Greek yogurt
- 2 tablespoons mayonnaise
- 1 tablespoon honey
- 1/2 teaspoon cinnamon
- Salt to taste

INSTRUCTIONS:
a) In a large bowl, combine pasta, diced apples, celery, walnuts, and raisins.
b) In a small bowl, mix together Greek yogurt, mayonnaise, honey, cinnamon, and a pinch of salt.
c) Pour the dressing over the pasta mixture and toss until well coated.
d) Refrigerate for at least 1 hour before serving.

93. Pineapple and Ham Pasta Salad

INGREDIENTS:
- 2 cups dried pasta, cooked and cooled
- 1 cup pineapple chunks
- 1/2 cup ham, diced
- 1/4 cup red bell pepper, diced
- 1/4 cup green onions, chopped
- 1/3 cup mayonnaise
- 2 tablespoons Dijon mustard
- 1 tablespoon honey
- Salt and pepper to taste

INSTRUCTIONS:
a) In a large bowl, combine pasta, pineapple chunks, diced ham, red bell pepper, and green onions.
b) In a small bowl, whisk together mayonnaise, Dijon mustard, honey, salt, and pepper.
c) Pour the dressing over the pasta mixture and toss until well coated.
d) Refrigerate for at least 1 hour before serving.

94. Citrus Berry Pasta Salad

INGREDIENTS:
- 2 cups bowtie pasta, cooked and cooled
- 1 cup mixed berries (strawberries, blueberries, raspberries)
- 1 orange, segmented
- 1/4 cup fresh mint, chopped
- 2 tablespoons honey
- 2 tablespoons orange juice
- 1 tablespoon lime juice
- Salt to taste

INSTRUCTIONS:
a) In a large bowl, combine pasta, mixed berries, orange segments, and fresh mint.
b) In a small bowl, whisk together honey, orange juice, lime juice, and a pinch of salt.
c) Pour the dressing over the pasta mixture and toss until well coated.
d) Refrigerate for at least 1 hour before serving.

95. Kiwi, Strawberry, and Rotini Pasta Salad

INGREDIENTS:
- 2 cups rotini pasta, cooked and cooled
- 1 cup strawberries, sliced
- 2 kiwis, peeled and diced
- 1/4 cup almonds, sliced and toasted
- 2 tablespoons poppy seed dressing
- 2 tablespoons Greek yogurt
- 1 tablespoon honey
- Salt to taste

INSTRUCTIONS:
a) In a large bowl, combine pasta, sliced strawberries, diced kiwis, and toasted almonds.
b) In a small bowl, whisk together poppy seed dressing, Greek yogurt, honey, and a pinch of salt.
c) Pour the dressing over the pasta mixture and toss until well coated.
d) Refrigerate for at least 1 hour before serving.

96. Mango Salsa with Farfalle Pasta Salad

INGREDIENTS:
- 2 cups farfalle pasta, cooked and cooled
- 1 mango, diced
- 1/2 cup black beans, rinsed and drained
- 1/4 cup red bell pepper, diced
- 1/4 cup red onion, finely chopped
- 2 tablespoons fresh cilantro, chopped
- 3 tablespoons lime juice
- 2 tablespoons olive oil
- 1 teaspoon cumin
- Salt and pepper to taste

INSTRUCTIONS:
a) In a large bowl, combine pasta, diced mango, black beans, red bell pepper, red onion, and cilantro.
b) In a small bowl, whisk together lime juice, olive oil, cumin, salt, and pepper.
c) Pour the dressing over the pasta mixture and toss until well coated.
d) Refrigerate for at least 1 hour before serving.

97. Peach and Prosciutto Pasta Salad

INGREDIENTS:
- 2 cups fusilli pasta, cooked and cooled
- 2 peaches, sliced
- 1/4 cup prosciutto, thinly sliced
- 1/2 cup mozzarella balls
- 1/4 cup red onion, finely chopped
- 3 tablespoons balsamic glaze
- 3 tablespoons olive oil
- Salt and pepper to taste

INSTRUCTIONS:
a) In a large bowl, combine pasta, sliced peaches, prosciutto, mozzarella balls, and red onion.
b) Drizzle with balsamic glaze and olive oil.
c) Toss until well combined.
d) Season with salt and pepper to taste.
e) Refrigerate for at least 1 hour before serving.

98. Blueberry and Goat Cheese Pasta Salad

INGREDIENTS:
- 2 cups penne pasta, cooked and cooled
- 1 cup blueberries
- 1/2 cup goat cheese, crumbled
- 1/4 cup almonds, sliced and toasted
- 2 tablespoons honey
- 2 tablespoons balsamic vinegar
- 3 tablespoons olive oil
- Salt and pepper to taste

INSTRUCTIONS:
a) In a large bowl, combine pasta, blueberries, goat cheese, and toasted almonds.
b) In a small bowl, whisk together honey, balsamic vinegar, olive oil, salt, and pepper.
c) Pour the dressing over the pasta mixture and toss until well coated.
d) Refrigerate for at least 1 hour before serving.

99. Spinach, Pea, Raspberry, and Spiral Pasta Salad

INGREDIENTS:
- 8 oz spiral pasta (tricolor or whole wheat for added color and nutrition)
- 2 cups fresh spinach leaves, washed and torn
- 1 cup fresh or frozen peas, blanched and cooled
- 1 cup fresh raspberries, washed
- 1/2 cup feta cheese, crumbled
- 1/4 cup red onion, finely chopped
- 1/4 cup chopped fresh mint leaves
- 1/4 cup chopped fresh basil leaves
- For the Dressing:
- 1/4 cup olive oil
- 2 tablespoons balsamic vinegar
- 1 tablespoon Dijon mustard
- 1 tablespoon honey
- Salt and pepper to taste

INSTRUCTIONS:
a) Cook the spiral pasta according to the package instructions. Drain and rinse with cold water to cool it down quickly. Set aside.

PREPARE THE DRESSING:
b) In a small bowl, whisk together the olive oil, balsamic vinegar, Dijon mustard, honey, salt, and pepper. Adjust the seasoning to taste.

ASSEMBLE THE SALAD:
c) In a large mixing bowl, combine the cooked and cooled spiral pasta, torn spinach leaves, blanched peas, raspberries, crumbled feta cheese, chopped red onion, mint, and basil.

d) Pour the dressing over the salad ingredients.

e) Gently toss the salad to ensure that all ingredients are well coated with the dressing. Be careful not to crush the raspberries.

f) Cover the salad bowl with plastic wrap and refrigerate for at least 30 minutes to allow the flavors to meld.

g) Before serving, give the salad a final gentle toss. You can garnish with extra mint leaves or a sprinkle of feta if desired.

100. Mandarin Orange and Almond Pasta Salad

INGREDIENTS:
- 2 cups rotini pasta, cooked and cooled
- 1 can (11 oz) mandarin oranges, drained
- 1/2 cup sliced almonds, toasted
- 1/4 cup green onions, chopped
- 3 tablespoons rice vinegar
- 2 tablespoons soy sauce
- 2 tablespoons sesame oil
- 1 tablespoon honey
- Salt and pepper to taste

INSTRUCTIONS:
a) In a large bowl, combine pasta, mandarin oranges, toasted almonds, and green onions.
b) In a small bowl, whisk together rice vinegar, soy sauce, sesame oil, honey, salt, and pepper.
c) Pour the dressing over the pasta mixture and toss until well coated.
d) Refrigerate for at least 1 hour before serving.

CONCLUSION

As the final pages of "Pasta Perfection: Cool Pasta Salads for Every Occasion" gracefully conclude, we hope your culinary journey through these irresistible pasta salads has been a delightful exploration of taste and creativity. This cookbook isn't just a guide; it's an ode to the art of crafting pasta salads that are not only visually appealing but also irresistibly delicious.

As you savor the last bites of these 100 pasta salad creations, remember that you've not just mastered recipes; you've embraced a culinary philosophy that celebrates the marriage of simplicity and sophistication. May your kitchen continue to be a space where creativity knows no bounds, and the pursuit of pasta perfection is a never-ending joy.

Until we meet again in your next culinary adventure, may your meals be filled with the spirit of crafting and savoring pasta perfection. Happy salad crafting!

www.ingramcontent.com/pod-product-compliance
Lightning Source LLC
Chambersburg PA
CBHW050351120526
44590CB00015B/1643